QUOTES BY SWAMI VIVEKANANDA

INSPIRING THOUGHTS FOR THE BEST YOU

TEAM INDUS

Copyright © Team Indus
All Rights Reserved.

ISBN 979-888546269-3

This book has been published with all efforts taken to make the material error-free after the consent of the author. However, the author and the publisher do not assume and hereby disclaim any liability to any party for any loss, damage, or disruption caused by errors or omissions, whether such errors or omissions result from negligence, accident, or any other cause.

While every effort has been made to avoid any mistake or omission, this publication is being sold on the condition and understanding that neither the author nor the publishers or printers would be liable in any manner to any person by reason of any mistake or omission in this publication or for any action taken or omitted to be taken or advice rendered or accepted on the basis of this work. For any defect in printing or binding the publishers will be liable only to replace the defective copy by another copy of this work then available.

Dedicated to the great visionary, scholar and thinker **Swami Vivekananda**

Contents

Team Indus   vii

Great Thoughts

Team Indus

A work by Team Indus of **Indusland Publications**

Great Thoughts

"Take up one idea. Make that one idea your life; dream of it; think of it; live on that idea. Let the brain, the body, muscles, nerves, every part of your body be full of that idea, and just leave every other idea alone. This is the way to success, and this is the way great spiritual giants are produced."

*"You have to grow from the inside out. None can teach you,
none can make you spiritual.
There is no other teacher but your own soul."*

"In a conflict between the heart and the brain, follow your heart."

"In a day, when you don't come across any problems - you can be sure that you are travelling in a wrong path"

"The great secret of true success, of true happiness, is this: the man or woman who asks for no return, the perfectly unselfish person, is the most successful."

"All power is within you; you can do anything and everything. Believe in that, do not believe that you are weak; do not believe that you are half-crazy lunatics, as most of us do nowadays. You can do any thing and everything, without even the guidance of any one. Stand up and express the divinity within you."

"The greatest religion is to be true to your own nature. Have faith in yourselves."

"The greatest sin is to think yourself weak"

"Anything that makes weak - physically, intellectually and spiritually, reject it as poison."

"Dare to be free, dare to go as far as your thought leads, and dare to carry that out in your life."

"We are what our thoughts have made us; so take care about what you think. Words are secondary. Thoughts live; they travel far."

"Be not Afraid of anything. You will do Marvelous work. it is Fearlessness that brings Heaven even in a moment."

"Arise, awake, stop not till the goal is reached."

"They alone live, who live for others."

"All love is expansion, all selfishness is contraction. Love is therefore the only law of life. He who loves lives, he who is selfish is dying. Therefore love for love's sake, because it is the only law of life, just as you breathe to live."

"You cannot believe in God until you believe in yourself."

"Neither seek nor avoid, take what comes."

"Strength is Life, Weakness is Death. Expansion is Life, Contraction is Death. Love is Life, Hatred is Death."

"Feel nothing, know nothing, do nothing, have nothing, give up all to God, and say utterly, 'Thy will be done.' We only dream this bondage. Wake up and let it go."

"Comfort is no test of truth. Truth is often far from being comfortable."

"The fire that warms us can also consume us; it is not the fault of the fire."

"Learn Everything that is Good from Others, but bring it in, and in your own way absorb it; do not become others."

"Was there ever a more horrible blasphemy than the statement that all the knowledge of God is confined to this or that book? How dare men call God infinite, and yet try to compress Him within the covers of a little book!"

"Do one thing at a Time, and while doing it put your whole Soul into it to the exclusion of all else."

"We are responsible for what we are, and whatever we wish ourselves to be, we have the power to make ourselves. If what we are now has been the result of our own past actions, it certainly follows that whatever we wish to be in the future can be produced by our present actions; so we have to know how to act."

*"whatever you think that you will be.
if you think yourself weak,weak you will be;
if you think yourself strong,you will be"*

"Ask nothing; want nothing in return. Give what you have to give; it will come back to you, but do not think of that now."

"All differences in this world are of degree, and not of kind, because oneness is the secret of everything."

"Each work has to pass through these stages—ridicule, opposition, and then acceptance. Those who think ahead of their time are sure to be misunderstood."

"A fool may buy all the books in the world, and they will be in his library; but he will be able to read only those that he deserves to."

*"We reap what we sow. We are the makers of our own fate.
The wind is blowing; those vessels whose sails are unfurled
catch it, and go forward on their way, but those which have
their sails furled do not catch the wind. Is that the fault of
the wind?....... We make our own destiny."*

"Condemn none: if you can stretch out a helping hand, do so. If you cannot, fold your hands, bless your brothers, and let them go their own way."

"Books are infinite in number and time is short. The secret of knowledge is to take what is essential. Take that and try to live up to it."

"beleive in yourself and the world will be at your feet"

"Never say, "O Lord, I am a miserable sinner." Who will help you? You are the help of the universe. What in this universe can help you? What can prevail over you? You are the God of the universe; where can you seek for help? Never help came from anywhere but from yourself. In your ignorance, every prayer that you made and that was answered, you thought was answered by some Being, but you answered the prayer yourself unknowingly. The help came from yourself, and you fondly imagined that someone was sending help to you. There is no help for you outside of yourself; you are the creator

of the universe. Like the silkworm, you have built a cocoon around yourself. Who will save you? Burst your own cocoon and come out as a beautiful butterfly, as the free soul. Then alone you will see Truth."

"All the powers in the universe are already ours. It is we who have put our hands before our eyes and cry that it is dark."

"The world is the great gymnasium where we come to make ourselves strong."

"The only religion that ought to be taught is the religion of fearlessness. Either in this world or in the world of religion, it is true that fear is the sure cause of degradation and sin. It is fear that brings misery, fear that brings death, fear that breeds evil. And what causes fear? Ignorance of our own nature."

"The whole life is a succession of dreams. My ambition is to be a conscious dreamer, that is all."

"Each soul is potentially divine. The goal is to manifest this divinity by controlling nature, external and internal. Do this either by work, or worship, or psychic control, or philosophy - by one, or more, or all of these - and be free. This is the whole of religion. Doctrines, or dogmas, or rituals, or books, or temples, or forms, are but secondary details."

"Take Risks in Your Life If u Win, U Can Lead! If u Lose, U Can Guide!"

"There is no God separate from you, no God higher than you, the real 'you'. All the gods are little beings to you, all the ideas of God and Father in heaven are but your own reflection. God Himself is your image. 'God created man after His own image.' That is wrong. Man creates God after his own image. That is right. Throughout the universe we are creating gods after our own image. We

create the god and fall down at his feet and worship him; and when this dream comes, we love it!"

"Education is the manifestation of perfection already existing in man."

"Shri Ramakrishna use to say, "As Long as I Live, so long do I learn". That man or that society which has nothing to learn is already in the jaws of death."

"The greatest truths are the simplest things in the world, simple as your own existence."

"Where can we go to find God if we cannot see Him in our own hearts and in every living being."

"Desire, ignorance, and inequality—this is the trinity of bondage."

"How often does a man ruin his disciples by remaining always with them! When men are once trained, it is essential that their leader leave them, for without his absence they cannot develop themselves. Plants always remain small under a big tree."

"Do not believe a thing because you have read about it in a book. Do not believe a thing because another man has said it was true. Do not believe in words because they are hallowed by tradition. Find out the truth for yourself. Reason it out. That is realization."

"There is no limit to the power of the human mind. The more concentrated it is, the more power is brought to bear on one point"

"All knowledge that the world has ever received comes from the mind; the infinite library of the universe is in our own mind."

"Things do not grow better; they remain as they are. It is we who grow better, by the changes we make in ourselves."

"Astrology and all these mystical things are generally signs of a weak mind; therefore as soon as they are becoming prominent in our minds, we should see a physician, take good food, and rest."

"You must worship the Self in Krishna, not Krishna as Krishna."

"The very reason for nature's existence is for the education of the soul."

"The brain and muscles must develop simultaneously. Iron nerves with an intelligent brain — and the whole world is at your feet."

"The cheerful mind perseveres and the strong mind hews its way through a thousand difficulties."

"The Vedanta recognizes no sin it only recognizes error. And the greatest error, says the Vedanta is to say that you are weak, that you are a sinner, a miserable creature, and that you have no power and you cannot do this and that."

"The powers of the mind are like the rays of the sun when they are concentrated they illumine."

"Give up the idea that by ruling over others you can do any good to them. But you can do just as much as you can in the case of the plant: you can supply the growing seed with the materials for the making

up of its body, bringing to it the earth, the water, the air, that it wants. It will take all that it wants by its own nature, it will assimilate and grow by its own nature."

"Be strong! ... You talk of ghosts and devils. We are the living devils. The sign of life is strength and growth. The sign of death is weakness. Whatever is weak, avoid! It is death. If it is strength, go down into hell and get hold of it! There is salvation only for the brave. "None but the brave deserves the fair." None but the bravest deserves salvation."

"He is an atheist who does not believe in himself. The old religions said that he was an atheist who did not believe in God. The new religion says that he is an atheist who does not believe in himself."

"So long as the millions live in hunger and ignorance, I hold every person a traitor who, having been educated at their expense, pays not the least heed to them!"

"The moment I have realized God sitting in the temple of every human body, the moment I stand in reverence before every human being and see God in him - that moment I am free from bondage, everything that binds vanishes, and I am free."

"Even the greatest fool can accomplish a task if it were after his or her heart. But the intelligent ones are those who can convert every work into one that suits their taste."

"Blessed are they whose bodies get destroyed in the service of others."

"Are you unselfish? That is the question. If you are, you will be perfect without reading a single religious book, without going into a single church or temple."

"Don't look back—forward, infinite energy, infinite enthusiasm, infinite daring, and infinite patience—then alone can great deeds be accomplished."

"Devotion to duty is the highest form of worship of God."

"Truth can be stated in a thousand different ways, yet each one can be true."

"Bless people when they revile you. Think how much good they are doing by helping to stamp out the false ego."

"The earth is enjoyed by heroes"—this is the unfailing truth. Be a hero. Always say, "I have no fear."

"This is a great fact: strength is life; weakness is death. Strength is felicity, life eternal, immortal; weakness is constant strain and misery, weakness is death."

"All truth is eternal. Truth is nobody's property; no race, no individual can lay any exclusive claim to it. Truth is the nature of all souls."

"Be not afraid of anything. You will do marvellous work. It is fear that is the great cause of misery in the world. It is fear that is the greatest of all superstitions. It is fear that is the cause of all our woes, and it is fearlessness that brings heaven even in a moment. Therefore, "arise, awake and stop not until the goal is reached."

"Man is to become divine by realizing the divine. Idols or temples, or churches or books, are only the supports, the help of his spiritual childhood."

"Liberty is the first condition of growth. It is wrong, a thousand times wrong, if any of you dares to say, 'I will work out the salvation of this woman or child."

"He who struggles is better than he who never attempts."

"If in this hell of a world one can bring a little joy and peace even for a day into the heart of a single person, that much alone is true; this I have learnt after suffering all my life; all else is mere moonshine. . . ."

"God did not give me everything that i wanted. But, He gave me everything that i needed!"

"The Tapas and the other hard Yogas that were practiced in other Yugas do not work now. What is needed in this Yuga is giving, helping others."

"The more we come out and do good to others, the more our hearts will be purified, and God will be in them."

"Do good because it is good to do good. Ask no more."

"You need not worry or make yourself sleepless about the world; it will go on without you."

"After every happiness comes misery; they may be far apart or near. The more advanced the soul, the more quickly does one follow the other. What we want is neither happiness nor misery. Both make us forget our true nature; both are chains--one iron, one gold; behind both is the Atman, who knows

neither happiness nor misery. These are states, and states must ever change; but the nature of the Atman is bliss, peace, unchanging. We have not to get it, we have it; only wash away the dross and see it."

"It is a very hard thing to understand, but you will come to learn in time that nothing in the universe has power over you until you allow it to exercise such a power."

---

*"The knowing ones must have pity on the ignorant. One who knows is willing to give up his body even for an ant,
because he knows that the body is nothing."*

"Do not believe in a thing because you have read about it in a book. Do not believe in a thing because another man has said it was true. Do not believe in words because they are hallowed by tradition. Find out the truth for yourself. Reason it out. That is realization."

"Desire can be eradicated from the roots by firmly imbibing the four attributes of: Jnan, Atmanishtha, Vairagya, Dharma and the full fledged devotion to God."

"The Buddhists or the Jains do not depend upon God; but the whole force of their religion is directed to the great central truth in every religion, to evolve a God out of man. They have not seen the Father, but they have seen the Son. And he that hath seen the Son hath seen the Father also."

"But there is yet time to change our ways. Give up all those old discussions, old fights about things which are meaningless, which are nonsensical in their very nature. Think of the last six hundred or seven hundred years of degradation when grown-up men by hundreds have been discussing for years whether we should drink a glass of water with the right hand or the left, whether the hand should be washed three times or four times, whether we should gargle five or six times. What can you expect from men who pass their lives in discussing

such momentous questions as these and writing most learned philosophies on them! There is a danger of our religion getting into the kitchen. We are neither Vedantists, most of us now, nor Pauranics, nor Tantrics. We are just "Don'ttouchists". Our religion is in the kitchen. Our God is the cooking-pot, and our religion is, "Don't touch me, I am holy". If this goes on for another century, every one of us will be in a lunatic asylum. It is a sure sign of softening of the brain when the mind cannot grasp the higher problems of life; all originality is lost, the mind has lost all its strength, its activity, and its power of thought, and just tries to go round and round the smallest curve it can find."

"The mother and the father are the causes of this body; so a man must undergo a thousand troubles in order to do good to them."

*"People laugh at me because I am different;
I laugh at people cause the are all the same."*

"If a man can realize his divine nature with the help of an image, would it be right to call that a sin? Nor, even when he has passed that stage, should he call it an error. [...] man is not traveling from error to truth, but from truth to truth, from lower to higher truth. To him all the religions from the lowest fetishism to the highest absolutism, mean so many attempts of the human soul to grasp and realize the Infinite, each determined by the conditions of its birth and association, and each of these marks a stage of progress; and every soul is a young eagle soaring higher and higher, gathering more and more strength till it reaches the Glorious Sun."

"This World will always continue to be a mixture of Good and Evil. Our duty is to sympathize with the weak and to Love even the wrongdoer."

"By doing well the duty which is nearest to us, the duty which is in our hands, we make ourselves stronger"

"This universe is the wreckage of the infinite on the shores of the finite."

"When an idea exclusively occupies the mind, it is transformed into an actual physical or mental state."

"Why should a Man be Moral? Because this strengthens his will."

Talk to yourself at least once in a Day, otherwise you may miss a meeting with an EXCELLENT person in this World."

"Be Grateful to the Man you help, think of Him as God. Is it not a great privilege to be allowed to worship God by helping our fellow men?"

"We must also remember that in every little village-god and every little superstitious custom is that which we are accustomed to call our religious faith. But local customs are infinite and contradictory. Which are we to obey, and which not to obey? The Brāhmin of Southern India, for instance, would shrink in horror at the sight of another Brahmin eating meat; a Brahmin in the North thinks it a most glorious and holy thing to do—he kills goats by the hundred in sacrifice. If you put forward your custom, they are equally ready with theirs. Various are the customs all over India, but they are local. The greatest mistake made is that ignorant people always think that this local custom is the essence of our religion."

"A good practice carried to an extreme and worked in accordance with the letter of the law becomes a positive evil."

"The help which tends to make us spiritually strong is the highest help, next to it comes intellectual help and after that comes physical help."

"Of one hundred persons who take up the spiritual life, eighty turn out to be charlatans, fifteen insane, and only five, maybe, get a glimpse of the real truth. Therefore beware."

"A few heart-whole, sincere, and energetic men and women can do more in a year than a mob in a century."

"Have Faith in Man, whether he appears to you to be a very learned one or a most ignorant one."

"The one great advantage of Bhakti is that it is the easiest and most natural way to reach the great divine end in view; it's great disadvantage is that in its lower forms it oftentimes degenerates into hideous fanaticism. The fanatical crew in Hinduism, Mohammedanism, or Christianity, have always been almost exclusively recruited from these worshippers [sic] on the lower planes of Bhakti. That singleness of attachment (Nishthâ) to a loved object, without which no genuine love can grow, is very often also the cause of the denunciation of

everything else. All the weak and undeveloped minds in every religion or country have only one way of loving their own ideal, i.e., by hating every other ideal. Herein is the explanation of why the same man who is so lovingly attached to his own ideal of God, so devoted to his own ideal of religion, becomes a howling fanatic as soon as he sees or hears anything of any other ideal."

"God Gave Me Nothing I Wanted He Gave Me Everything I Needed."

"The goal of mankind is knowledge. That is the one ideal placed before us by Eastern philosophy. Pleasure is not the goal of man, but knowledge. Pleasure and happiness come to an end. It is a mistake to suppose that pleasure is the goal."

"Our duty is to encourage every one in his struggle to live up to his own highest idea, and strive at the same time to make the ideal as near as possible to the Truth."

"The will is not free - it is a phenomenon bound by cause and effect - but there is something behind the will which is free."

"Ignorance is the mother of all the evil and all the misery we see. Let men have light, let them be pure and spiritually strong and educated, then alone will misery cease in the world, not before. We may convert every house in the country into a charity asylum, we may fill the land with hospitals, but the misery of man will still continue to exist until man's character changes."

"The tender plant of spirituality will die if exposed too early to the action of a constant change of ideas and ideals. Many people, in the name of what may be called religious liberalism, may be seen feeding their idle curiosity with a continuous succession of different ideals. With them, hearing new things grows into a kind of disease, a sort of religious drink-mania. They want to hear new things just by way of getting a temporary nervous excitement, and when one such exciting influence has had its

effect on them, they are ready for another. Religion is with these people a sort of intellectual opium-eating, and there it ends."

"The mind is in its own nature when it is calm. The moment you can calm it, that [very] moment you will know the truth."

"The Heart and core of everything here is good, that whatever may be the surface waves, deep down and underlying everything, there is an infinite basis of Goodness and Love."

"The Older I grow, the more everything seems to me to lie in manliness. This is my new gospel"

"The human mind is like that monkey, incessantly active by its own nature; then it becomes drunk with the wine of desire, thus increasing its turbulence. After desire takes possession comes the

sting of the scorpion of jealousy at the success of others, and last of all the demon of pride enters the mind, making it think itself of all importance."

"A tremendous stream is flowing toward the ocean, carrying us all along with it; and though like straws and scraps of paper we may at times float aimlessly about, in the long run we are sure to join the Ocean of Life and Bliss."

"We only know the universe from the point of view of beings with five senses. Suppose we obtain another sense, the whole universe must change for us."

"If the Student thinks he is the Spirit, he will be a better Student. If the Lawyer thinks he is the Spirit, he will be a better Lawyer, and so on."

"Never forget the glory of human nature! We are the greatest god.. Christs and Buddhas are but waves in the boundless ocean which I AM."

"Where the whole world is awake, the sage sleeps."

"The ideal man is he who, in the midst of the greatest silence and solitude, finds the intensest activity, and in the midst of the intensest activity finds the silence and solitude of the desert."

"If a man works without any selfish motive in view, does he not gain anything? Yes, he gains the highest. Unselfishness is more paying, only people have not the patience to practice it. It is more paying from the point of view of health also. Love, truth, and unselfishness are not merely moral figures of speech, but they form our highest ideal, because in them lies such a manifestation of power. In the first place, a man who can work for five days, or even for five minutes, without any selfish motive whatever, without thinking of future, of heaven, of punishment, or anything of the kind, has

in him the capacity to become a powerful moral giant. It is hard to do it, but in the heart of our hearts we know its value, and the good it brings. It is the greatest manifestation of power — this tremendous restraint; self-restraint is a manifestation of greater power than all outgoing action."

"Never think there is anything impossible for the soul. It is the greatest heresy to think so. If there is sin, this is the only sin; to say that you are weak, or others are weak."

"A little of the infinite is projected into consciousness, and that we call our world."

"The more we grow in Love, Virtue and Holiness, the more we see Love, Virtue and Holiness outside."

"This attachment of Love to God is indeed one that does not bind the soul but effectively breaks all its bondages."

"If you [can realise Brahman] by standing on your head, or on one foot, or by worshipping five thousand gods with three heads each — welcome to it! ... Do it any way you can! Nobody has any right to say anything. Therefore, Krishna says, if your method is better and higher, you have no business to say that another man's method is bad, however wicked you may think it."

"The Christian is not to become a Hindu or a Buddhist, nor is a Hindu or a Buddhist to become a Christian. But each must assimilate the spirit of the others and yet preserve his individuality and grow according to his own law of growth. If the Parliament of Religions has shown anything to the world, it is this: It has proved to the world that holiness, purity, and charity are not the exclusive possessions of any church in the world, and that every system has produced men and women of the most exalted character. In the face of this evidence, if anybody dreams of the exclusive survival of his own religion at the expense of the others, I pity him

from the bottom of my heart and point out to him that upon the banner of every religion will soon be written, in spite of resistance: "Help and not Fight," "Assimilation and not Destruction," "Harmony and Peace and not Dissension"."

"Now is wanted intense Karma-Yoga with unbounded courage and indomitable strength in the heart. Then only will the people of the country be roused."

"It is better not to love, if loving only means hating others. That is no love. That is hell! If loving your own people means hating everybody else, it is the quintessence of selfishness and brutality, and the effect is that it will make you brutes. Therefore, better die working out your own natural religion than following another's natural religion, however great it may appear to you"

"If faith in ourselves had been more extensively taught and practiced, I am sure a very large portion of the evils and miseries that we have would have

vanished."

"God is present in every Jiva; there is no other God besides that. Who serves Jiva serves God indeed."

"there is a continuity of mind, as the Yogis call it. The mind is universal. Your mind, my mind, all these little minds, are fragments of that universal mind, little waves in the ocean; and"

"But where the ignorant are asleep, there the sage keeps awake"

"As all the rivers of the world constantly pour their waters into the ocean, but the ocean's grand, majestic nature remains undisturbed and unchanged,"

"Take up one idea. Make that one idea your life; dream of it; think of it; live on that idea. Let the brain, the body, muscles, nerves, every part of your body be full of that idea, and just leave every other idea alone. This is the way to success, and this is the way great spiritual giants are produced."
— Swami Vivekananda, Vedanta Philosophy: Lectures by the Swami Vivekananda on Raja Yoga Also Pantanjali's Yoga Aphorisms, with Commentaries, and Glossary of Sa"

"Later on we read what Krishna says, "Even those who worship other deities are really worshipping me" (note 31). It is God incarnate whom man is worshipping. Would God be angry if you called Him by the wrong name? He would be no God at all! Can't you understand that whatever a man has in his own heart is God — even if he worships a stone? What of that! We will understand more clearly if we once get rid of the idea that religion consists in doctrines. One idea of religion has been that the whole world was born because Adam ate the apple, and there is no way of escape. Believe in Jesus Christ — in a certain man's death! But in India there is quite a different idea. [There] religion means realisation, nothing else. It does not matter whether one approaches the destination in a carriage with four horses, in an electric car, or

rolling on the ground. The goal is the same. For the [Christians] the problem is how to escape the wrath of the terrible God. For the Indians it is how to become what they really are, to regain their lost Selfhood. ..."

"The great men think, and you and I [also] think. But there is a difference. We think and our bodies do not follow. Our actions do not harmonise with our thoughts. Our words have not the power of the words that become Vedas. ... Whatever they think must be accomplished. If they say, "I do this," the body does it. Perfect obedience. This is the end. You can think yourself God in one minute, but you cannot be [God]."

"Stand alone! See the glory of your own soul, and see that you will have to work."

"When the body is sufficiently controlled, we can attempt the manipulation of the mind."

"All condemnation of others really condemns ourselves. Adjust the microcosm which is in your power to do) and the macrocosm will adjust itself for you."

"Religion is being and becoming. Religion is the manifestation of the Divinity already in man."

"Above all, beware of compromises. I do not mean that you are to get into antagonism with anybody, but you have to hold on to your own principles in weal or woe and never adjust them to others' "fads" through the greed of getting supporters. Your Atman is the support of the universe—whose support do you stand in need of?"

"Be not afraid, for all great power throughout the history of humanity has been with the people. From out of their ranks have come all the greatest geniuses of the world, and history can only repeat itself. Be not afraid of anything. You will do marvelous work."

"The Gita is a commentary on the Upanishads. The Upanishads are the Bible of India."

"All the powers in the universe are already ours."

"There was never a time when we did not exist."

"There will never be a time when we shall not exist."

"Tell your body that it is strong, tell your mind that it is strong, and have unbounded faith and hope in yourself."

"Put the good before them, see how eagerly they take it, see how the divine that never dies, that is always living in the human..."

"If money help a man to do good to others, it is of some value; but if not, it is simply a mass of evil, and the sooner it is got rid of, the better."

"No knowledge comes from outside; it is all inside. What we say a man "knows", should, in strict psychological language, be what he "discovers" or "unveils"; what a man "learns" is really what he "discovers", by taking the cover off his own soul, which is a mine of infinite knowledge."

"Although a man has not studied a single system of philosophy, although he does not believe in any God, and never has believed, although he has not prayed even once in his whole life, if the simple power of good actions has brought him to that state where he is ready to give up his life and all else for others, he has arrived at the same point to which the religious man will come through his prayers and

the philosopher through his knowledge; and so you may find that the philosopher, the worker, and the devotee, all meet at one point, that one point being self-abnegation."

"You have to grow from the inside out. None can teach you, none can make you spiritual. There is no other teacher but your own soul."

"The present is determined by our past actions, and the future by the present."

"It is the Level-headed Man, the Calm Man, of Good Judgement and cool nerves, of Great sympathy and love, who does good work and so does good to himself."

"One infinite - pure and holy - beyond thoughts and beyond qualities - bow down to thee"

"The next step is Asana, posture. A series of exercises, physical and mental, is to be gone through every day, until certain higher states are reached. Therefore it is quite necessary that we should find a posture in which we can remain long. That posture which is the easiest for one should be the one chosen."

"As different streams having different sources all mingle their waters in the sea, so different tendencies, various though they appear, crooked or straight, all lead to God."

"Pranayama. Stopping the right nostril with the thumb, through the left nostril fill in air, according to capacity; then, without any interval, throw the air out through the right nostril, closing the left one. Again inhaling through the right nostril eject through the left, according to capacity; practicing this three or five times at four hours of the day, before dawn, during midday, in the evening, and at midnight, in fifteen days or a month purity of the nerves is attained; then begins Pranayama."

"MIND is not a dustbin to keep anger, hatred and jealousy. But it is the treasure box to keep, love happiness and sweet memories."

"It is the greatest manifestation of power to be calm. It is easy to be active. Let the reins go, and the horses will run away with you. Anyone can do that, but he who can stop the plunging horses is the strong man."

"We are like the caterpillar which takes the thread out of his own body and of that makes the cocoon, and behold, he is caught."

"My Faith is in the Younger Generation, the Modern Generation, out of them will come my workers. They will work out the whole problem, like Lions."

"Absolute equality, that which means a perfect balance of all the struggling forces in all the planes, can never be in this world. Before you attain that state, the world will have become quite unfit for any kind of life, and no one will be there. We find, therefore, that all these ideas of the millennium and of absolute equality are not only impossible but also that, if we try to carry them out, they will lead us surely enough to the day of destruction."

"The idea is, when a man receives a gift from another, his heart becomes impure, he becomes low, he loses his independence, he becomes bound and attached."

"THE WHOLE LIFE IS A SUCCESSION OF DREAMS; MY AMBITION IS TO BE A CONSCIOUS DREAMER, THATS ALL."

"You can not believe in god until you believe in yourself."

"Just as in the case of electricity, the modern theory is that the power leaves the dynamo and completes the circle back to the dynamo, so with hate and love; they must come back to the source. Therefore do not hate anybody, because that hatred which comes out from you, must, in the long run, come back to you. If you love, that love will come back to you, completing the circle."

"When you step beyond thought and intellect and all reasoning, then you have made the first step towards God; and that is the beginning of life."

"Curiously enough, it seems that at times the spiritual side prevails, and then the materialistic side—in wave-like motions following each other. ...At one time the full flood of materialistic ideas prevails, and everything in this life—prosperity, the education which procures more pleasures, more food—will become glorious at first and then that will degrade and degenerate. Along with the prosperity will rise to white heat all the inborn jealousies and hatreds of the human race.

Competition and merciless cruelty will be the watchword of the day. To quote a very commonplace and not very elegant English proverb, "Everyone for himself, and the devil take the hindmost", becomes the motto of the day. Then people think that the whole scheme of life is a failure. And the world would be destroyed had not spirituality come to the rescue and lent a helping hand to the sinking world. Then the world gets new hope and finds a new basis for a new building, and another wave of spirituality comes, which in time again declines. As a rule, spirituality brings a class of men who lay exclusive claim to the special powers of the world. The immediate effect of this is a reaction towards materialism, which opens the door to scores of exclusive claims, until the time comes when not only all the spiritual powers of the race, but all its material powers and privileges are centered in the hands of a very few; and these few, standing on the necks of the masses of the people, want to rule them. Then society has to help itself, and materialism comes to the rescue."

"What right has a man to say he has a soul if he does not feel it, or that there is a God if he does not see Him? If there is a God we must see Him, if there is a soul we must perceive it; otherwise it is better not to believe. It is better to be an outspoken

atheist than a hypocrite."

"GOD is to be worshipped as the one beloved, dearer than everything in this and next life."

"What is now wanted is a combination of the greatest heart with the highest intellectuality, of infinite love with infinite knowledge."

"Though our castes and institutions are apparently linked with our religion, they are not so. These institutions have been necessary to protect us as a nation, and when this necessity for self-preservation will no more exist, they will die a natural death. But the older I grow, the better I seem to think of these time-honored institutions of India. There was a time when I used to think that many of them were useless and worthless; but the older I grew, the more I seem to feel a diffidence in cursing any one of them, for each one of them is the embodiment of the experience of centuries. A child of but yesterday, destined to die the day after tomorrow, comes to me and asks me to change all

my plans; and if I hear the advice of that baby and change all my surroundings according to his ideas, I myself should be a fool, and no one else. Much of the advice that is coming to us from different countries is similar to this. Tell these wiseacres: "I will hear you when you have made a society yourselves. You cannot hold on to one idea for two days, you quarrel and fail; you are born like moths in the spring and die like them in five minutes. You come up like bubbles and burst like bubbles too. First form a stable society like ours. First make laws and institutions that remain undiminished in their power through scores of centuries. Then will be the time to talk on the subject with you, but till then, my friend, you are only a giddy child."

"He works for work's sake. "Work for work's sake. Worship for worship's sake."

"All who have actually attained any real religious experience never wrangle over the form in which the different religions are expressed. They know that the soul of all religions is the same and so they have no quarrel with anybody just because he or she does not speak in the same tongue."

"Anything that brings spiritual, mental, or physical weakness, touch it not with the toes of your feet."

"Krishna preached in the midst of the battlefield."

"It is a weakness to think that any one is dependent on me, and that I can do good to another. This belief is the mother of all our attachment, and through this attachment comes all our pain. We must inform our minds that no one in this universe depends upon us; not one beggar depends on our charity; not one soul on our kindness; not one living thing on our help. All are helped on by nature, and will be so helped even though millions of us were not here. The course of nature will not stop for such as you and me; it is, as already pointed out, only a blessed privilege to you and to me that we are allowed, in the way of helping others, to educate ourselves. This is a great lesson to learn in life, and when we have learned it fully, we shall never be unhappy; we can go and mix without harm in society anywhere and everywhere."

"No man is to be judged by the mere nature of his duties, but all should be judged by the manner and the spirit in which they perform them."

"He is trying to justify himself, but he cannot fool Krishna."

"The ideal man is he who, in the midst of the greatest silence and solitude, finds the intensest activity, and in the midst of the intensest activity finds the silence and solitude of the desert. He has learnt the secret of restraint, he has controlled himself."

"The sages of the world have only the right to tell us that they have analysed their minds and have found these facts, and if we do the same we shall also believe, and not before."

"Anything that is secret and mysterious in these systems of Yoga should be at once rejected. The best guide in life is strength. In religion, as in all other matters, discard everything that weakens you, have nothing to do with it."

"all religions alike, from the lowest fetishism to the highest absolutism, are but so many attempts of the human soul to grasp and realise the Infinite."

"We may talk and reason all our lives, but we shall not understand a word of truth, until we experience it ourselves."

"Just as inequality is necessary for creation itself, so the struggle to limit it is also necessary. If there were no struggle to become free and get back to God, there would be no creation either. It is the difference between these two forces that determines the nature of the motives of men. There will always be these motives to work, some tending

towards bondage and others towards freedom. This"

"We tend to reduce everyone else to the limits of our own mental universe and begin privileging our own ethics, morality, sense of duty and even our sense of utility. All religious conflicts arose from this propensity to judge others. If we indeed must judge at all, argued Vivekananda, then it must be `according to his own ideal, and not by that of anyone else'. It was important, therefore, to learn to look at the duty of others through their own eyes and never judge the customs and observances of others through the prism of our own standards."

"Let miseries come in millions of rivers and happiness in hundreds! I am no slave to misery! I am no slave to happiness!"

"The natural ambition of woman is through marriage to climb up, leaning upon a man; but those days are gone. You shall be great without the help of any man, just as you are."

"We are allowed to worship him. Stand in that reverent attitude to the whole universe, and then will come perfect non attachment"

"We have always heard it preached, „Love one another". What for? That doctrine was peached, but the explanation is here. Why should I love every one? Because they and I are one. Why should I love my brother? Because he and I are one. There is this oneness; this solidarity of the whole universe. From the lowest worm that crawls under our feet to the highest beings that ever lived – all have various bodies, but are the one Soul."

"man may see a great deal of difference between grass and a little tree, but if you mount very high, the grass and the biggest tree will appear much the same. So, from the standpoint of the highest ideal, the lowest animal and the highest man are the same. If"

"The man who thinks that he is receiving response to his prayers does not know that the fulfillment comes from his own nature, that he has succeeded by the mental attitude of prayer in waking up a bit of this infinite power which is coiled up within himself. What, thus, men ignorantly worship under various names, through fear and tribulation, the Yogi declares to the world to be the real power coiled up in every being, the mother of eternal happiness, if we but know how to approach her. And Raja-Yoga is the science of religion, the rationale of all worship, all prayers, forms, ceremonies, and miracles."

"We can read all the Vedas, and yet will not realize anything, but when we practice their teachings, then we attain to that state which realizes what the scriptures say, which penetrates where neither reason nor perception nor inference can go, and where the testimony of others cannot avail."

"Work for work's sake. There are some who are really the salt of the earth in every country and who work for work's sake, who do not care for name, or fame, or even to go to heaven."

"We must be Bright and Cheerful, long faces do not make Religion"

"A fool may buy all the books in the world, and they will be in his library; but he will be able to read only those that he deserves to; and this deserving is produced by Karma."

"If the Parliament of Religions has shown anything to the world it is this: It has proved to the world that holiness, purity and charity are not the exclusive possessions of any church in the world, and that every system has produced men and women of the most exalted character. In the face of this evidence, if anybody dreams of the exclusive survival of his own religion and the destruction of the others, I pity him from the bottom of my heart, and point out to him that upon the banner of every religion will soon be written, in spite of resistance: "Help and not Fight," "Assimilation and not Destruction," "Harmony and Peace and not Dissension."

"The Yogis say that the man who has discriminating powers, the man of good sense, sees through all that are called pleasure and pain, and knows that they come to all, and that one follows and melts into the other; he sees that men follow an ignis fatuus all their lives, and never succeed in fulfilling their desires. The great King Yudhishthira once said that the most wonderful thing in life is that evry moment we see people dying around us, and yet we think we shall never die. Surrounded by fools on every side, we think we are the only exceptions, the only learned men. Surrounded by all sorts of experiences of fickleness, we think our love is the only lasting love. How can that be? Even love is selfish, and the Yogi says that in the end we shall find that even the love of husbands and wives, children and friends, slowly decays. Decadence seizes everything in this life. It is only when everything, even love, fails, that, with a flash, man finds out how vain, how dreamlike is this world. Then he catches a glimpse of Vairagya, catches a glimpse of the beyond. It is only by giving up this world that the other comes; never through holding on to this one."

"Vairâgya or renunciation is the turning point in all the various Yogas. The Karmi (worker) renounces the fruits of his work. The Bhakta (devotee) renounces all little loves for the almighty and omnipresent love. The Yogi renounces his experiences, because his philosophy is that the whole Nature, although it is for the experience of the soul, at last brings him to know that he is not in Nature, but eternally separate from Nature. The Jnâni (philosopher) renounces everything, because his philosophy is that Nature never existed, neither in the past, nor present, nor will It in the future."

"Say, "This misery that I am suffering is of my own doing, and that very thing proves that it will have to be undone by me alone." That which I created, I can demolish; that which is created by some one else I shall never be able to destroy. Therefore, stand up, be bold, be strong. Take the whole responsibility on your own shoulders, and know that you are the creator of your own destiny. All the strength and succour you want is within yourselves. Therefore, make your own future. "Let the dead past bury its dead." The infinite future is before you, and you must always remember that each word, thought, and deed, lays up a store for you and that as the bad thoughts and bad works are ready to spring upon you like tigers, so also there is the

inspiring hope that the good thoughts and good deeds are ready with the power of a hundred thousand angels to defend you always and for ever. (II. 225)"

"You may sit down and listen to me by the hour every day, but if you do not practice, you will not get one step further. It all depends on practice."

"To the Hindu, says Vivekananda, "Man is not travelling from error to truth, but climbing up from truth to truth, from truth that is lower to truth that is higher."

"Our Karma determines what we deserve and what we can assimilate."

"the easiest way to make ourselves happy is to see that others are happy."

"What is it that is whirling the mind? Imagination, creative activity. Stop creation and you know the truth. All power of creation must stop, and then you know the truth at once."

"He who has no faith in himself can never have faith in God."

"When by analyzing his own mind, man comes face to face, as it were, with something which is never destroyed, something which is, by its own nature, eternally pure and perfect, he will no more be miserable, no more unhappy."

"To succeed, you must have tremendous perseverance, tremendous will. "I will drink the ocean," says the persevering soul, "at my will mountains will crumble up." Have that sort of energy, that sort of will, work hard, and you will reach the goal."

"You may ask, "Who wrote the Vedas?" They were not written. The words are the Vedas. A word is Veda, if I can pronounce it rightly. Then it will immediately produce the [desired] effect."

"If there is something here that is not in the Vedas, that is your delusion. It does not exist."

"Every work that we do, every movement of the body, every thought that we think, leaves such an impression on the mind-stuff, and even when such impressions are not obvious on the surface, they are sufficiently strong to work beneath the surface, subconsciously. What we are every moment is determined by the sum total of these impressions on the mind."

"The ideal of all education, all training, should be this man-making. But, instead of that, we are always trying to polish up the outside. What use in

polishing up the outside when there is no inside? The end and aim of all training is to make the man grow. The man who influences, who throws his magic, as it were, upon his fellow-beings, is a dynamo of power, and when that man is ready, he can do anything and everything he likes; that personality put upon anything will make it work."

"It is our own mental attitude which makes the world what it is for us. Our thoughts make things beautiful, our thoughts make things ugly. The whole world is in our own minds. Learn to see things in the proper light."

"Each soul is potentially divine. The goal is to manifest this Divinity within by controlling nature, external and internal. Do this either by work, or worship, or psychic control, or philosophy - by one, or more, or all of these -- and be free. This is the whole of religion. Doctrines, or dogmas, or rituals, or books, or temples, or forms, are but secondary details."

"you are all bound by the law of Karma, the Upanishads admit, but they declare the way out."

"Realisation is real religion, all the rest is only preparation — hearing lectures, or reading books, or reasoning is merely preparing the ground; it is not religion."

"Hindu religion does not consist in struggles and attempts to believe a certain doctrine or dogma, but in realising — not in believing, but in being and becoming."

"The Land where humanity has attained its highest towards gentleness, towards generosity, towards purity, towards calmness - it is India."

"Circumstances can never be good or bad. Only the individual man can be good or bad."

*"The whole secret of existence is to have no fear.
Never fear what will become of you, depend on no
one. Only the moment you reject all help are you
free."*

*"Can infinity have parts? What is meant by parts
of infinity? If you reason it out, you will find that it
is impossible. Infinity cannot be divided, it always
remains infinite. If it could be divided, each part
would be infinite. And there cannot be two
infinites. Suppose there were, one would limit the
other, and both would be finite. Infinity can only be
one, undivided. Thus the conclusion will be reached
that the infinite is one and not many, and that one
Infinite Soul is reflecting itself through thousands
and thousands of mirrors, appearing as so many
different souls. It is the same Infinite Soul, which is
the background of the universe, that we call God.
The same Infinite Soul also is the background of
the human mind which we call the human soul."*

*"Buddha is the only prophet who said, "I do not
care to know your various theories about God.
What is the use of discussing all the subtle*

doctrines about the soul? Do good and be good. And this will take you to freedom and to whatever truth there is." He was, in the conduct of his life, absolutely without personal motives; and what man worked more than he? Show me in history one character who has soared so high above all. The whole human race has produced but one such character, such high philosophy, such wide sympathy. This great philosopher, preaching the highest philosophy, yet had the deepest sympathy for the lowest of animals, and never put forth any claims for himself. He is the ideal Karma-Yogi, acting entirely without motive, and the history of humanity shows him to have been the greatest man ever born; beyond compare the greatest combination of heart and brain that ever existed, the greatest soul-power that has even been manifested. He is the first great reformer the world has seen. He was the first who dared to say, "Believe not because some old manuscripts are produced, believe not because it is your national belief, because you have been made to believe it from your childhood; but reason it all out, and after you have analysed it, then, if you find that it will do good to one and all, believe it, live up to it, and help others to live up to it." He works best who works without any motive, neither for money, nor for fame, nor for anything else; and when a man can do that, he will be a Buddha, and out of him will come the power to work in such a manner as will transform the world. This man represents the very highest ideal of Karma-Yoga."

"Why is there so much disturbance, so much fighting and quarrelling in the name of God? There has been more bloodshed in the name of God than for any other cause, because people never went to the fountain-head; they were content only to give a mental assent to the customs of their forefathers, and wanted others to do the same. What right has a man to say he has a soul if he does not feel it, or that there is a God if he does not see Him? If there is a God we must see Him, if there is a soul we must perceive it; otherwise it is better not to believe. It is better to be an outspoken atheist than a hypocrite."

"For all of us in this world life is a continuous fight."

"Many a time comes when we want to interpret our weakness and cowardice as forgiveness and renunciation."

"Who is the seer? The Self of man, the Purusha. What is the scene? The whole of nature beginning with the mind, down to gross matter."

"If you project hatred and jealousy, they will rebound on you with compound interest. No power can avert them; when once you have put them in motion, you will have to bear them. Remembering this will prevent you from doing wicked things."

"so even though all the senses bring in sensations from nature, the ocean-like heart of the sage knows no disturbance, knows no fear"

"Karma means law, and it applies everywhere. Everything is bound by Karma."

"Do not criticise others, for all doctrines and all dogmas are good; but show them by your lives that religion is no matter of books and beliefs, but of spiritual realisation."

"As such he cannot experience the nature of the soul. ..."

"When this Sushumna current opens, and begins to rise, we get beyond the senses, our minds become supersensuous, superconscious -- we get beyond even the intellect,"

"All weakness, all bondage is imagination."

"[Krishna answers:] "The man who has given up all desires, who desires nothing, not even this life, nor freedom, nor gods, nor work, nor anything."

"Even if you have knowledge, do not disturb the childlike faith of the ignorant. On the other hand, go down to their level and gradually bring them up (note 30). That is a very powerful idea, and it has become the ideal in India. That is why you can see a great philosopher going into a temple and worshipping images. It is not hypocrisy."

"When he has become perfectly satisfied, he has no more cravings"

"Only what is done as duty for duty's sake ... can scatter the bondage of Karma"

"Let us not be caught this time. So many times Maya has caught us, so many times have we exchanged our freedom for sugar dolls which melted when the water touched them. Don't be deceived. Maya is a great cheat. Get out. Do not let her catch you this time. Do not sell your priceless heritage for such delusions. Arise, awake, stop not till the goal is reached."

"and has found that the world, and the gods, and heaven are ... within his own Self."

"This is the sage who always works for work's sake without caring for the results."

"Thus he goes beyond the pain of birth and death. Thus he becomes free"

"The whole universe is only the self with variations, one tune made bearable by variations. Sometimes there are discords, but they only make the subsequent harmony more perfect."

"If you really want to judge of the character of a man, look not at his great performances. Every fool may become a hero at one time or another. Watch a man do his most common actions; those are

indeed the things which will tell you the real character of a great man. Great occasions rouse even the lowest of human beings to some kind of greatness, but he alone is the really great man whose character is great always, the same wherever he be."

"If you want to be religious, enter not the gate of any organised religions. They do a hundred times more evil than good, because they stop the growth of each one's individual development."

"The organs are the horses, the mind is the rein, the intellect is the charioteer, the soul is the rider, and the body is the chariot. The master of the household, the King, the Self of man, is sitting in this chariot."

"There is nothing holier in the world than to keep good company, because the good impressions will then tend to come to the surface."

"Mentally repeat: Let all beings be happy; Let all beings be peaceful; Let all beings be blissful. So do to the east, south, north and west. The more you do that the better you will feel yourself. You will find at last that the easiest way to make ourselves healthy is to see that others are healthy, and the easiest way to make ourselves happy is to see that others are happy. After doing that, those who believe in God should pray — not for money, not for health, nor for heaven; pray for knowledge and light; every other prayer is selfish."

"we have to bear the result of our own actions because we attach ourselves to them. ..."

"

Indusland Publications

www.ingramcontent.com/pod-product-compliance
Lightning Source LLC
LaVergne TN
LVHW010603070526
838199LV00063BA/5059